3

Gravel has a one in ten chance of dropping flint instead of a gravel block when broken. This applies to both naturally generated gravel and gravel placed by the player.

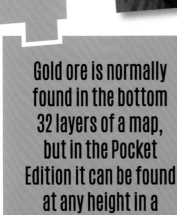

4

Gold ore is normally found in the bottom 32 layers of a map, but in the Pocket Edition it can be found at any height in a mesa biome.

5

Stone in Minecraft is an igneous rock, because it's formed when lava cools (usually in water).

6

Cobblestone is one of the most useful blocks in the game, featuring in 19 recipes!

7

Grass blocks attract passive mobs more than dim light. However, mobs will favour the bright light of torches, lanterns and fire.

8

Sheep can eat the grass off blocks to replenish their wool, turning them into dirt blocks. Luckily, the grass grows back!

9

Grass paths, currently only in the Pocket Edition but being added to the PC version, have flattened tops (making them slightly shorter than the full block height) and appear in villages that spawn on plains.

Coarse dirt can be made by mixing two gravel and two dirt blocks, and generates in high mountains and mega taiga. Grass can't grow on coarse dirt.

10

11

Farmland turns back into dirt if you jump on it too many times, if it's covered by another block, or if it dries out for too long.

Podzol and mycelium can't be crafted but can be collected from mega taiga and mushroom island biomes with a silk touch shovel. They both grow mushrooms in sunlight.

12

13

Despite their similarities, mycelium and podzol are slightly different: mycelium spreads to other dirt blocks, but podzol doesn't.

14

Mycelium and podzol can't be tilled with a hoe to make farmland. Coarse dirt turns into normal dirt if tilled and can then be turned into farmland.

15

Bedrock is the only naturally generated block in the game that can't be destroyed or collected.

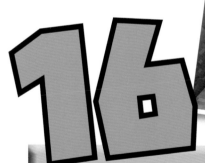

16

In older versions (and creative mode), it was possible to destroy bedrock. In a very early version, it took 16 minutes to break one piece, and in another version it turned to lava if exposed to sunlight!

In the Nether, bedrock forms a ceiling as well as a floor. It will burn forever if set on fire, just like Netherrack does.

17

18

When your top half is submerged in water and you're standing on something, blocks take five times longer to break than when on land.

19 If you're not standing on something (that is, sinking or swimming), blocks take 25 times as long to break while you're underwater!

20

While you're underwater, your field of vision shrinks by ten, so you can see slightly less on the outer edges. Watch out for attacks from the side!

21

Even though it's a liquid, you can't drown in lava, although it takes a lot of potions and enchanted armour pieces to test this theory!

22

Remember that you can sprint straight over one-block gaps without stopping.

23

Walking up stairs is faster than jumping up a slope. Craft stairs to make things easier for yourself!

24

Jack 'o' lanterns and glowstones emit light even underwater.

In the Console Edition of Minecraft, you can't place lava near the spawn point because this could kill you every time you respawn, breaking the map.

If you collect coal ore (for example, with a silk touch pickaxe), you can smelt it into coal, although this isn't very efficient because it uses coal to make coal!

Wood planks can be used as fuel in furnaces, which burn as long as wood, but as one wood block can be crafted into four planks, it's more efficient to burn planks.

28 Destroying a leaf block drops a sapling one in every 20 times. Jungle leaves only drop a sapling one in every 40 times, and oak leaves drop an apple one in every 200 times.

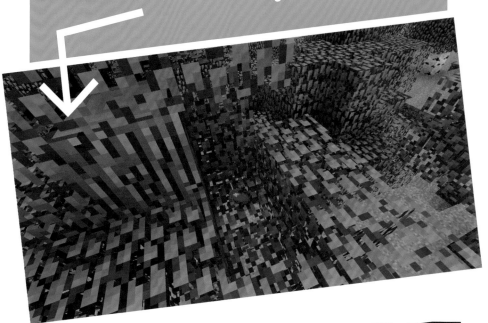

Chiselled sandstone can be made by combining two sandstone slabs. Yellow chiselled sandstone depicts a creeper face; red chiselled sandstone the wither! **29**

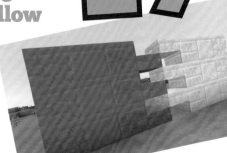

30

Diamond ore can generate in veins diagonally, so if you find some excavate around the entire block to make sure you haven't missed any!

31

Redstone ore gives off low-level light (9) for about a minute if struck or walked over. Sneaking as you contact it will stop this from happening.

Snow layers can be stacked to create partial blocks. Eight layers create a full-size snow block, also made by crafting together four snowballs.

Ice blocks cause you to slide, so if you sprint and hop you can travel across them twice as fast as riding in a full-speed minecart!

34 Both ice and snow blocks melt if placed near a strong enough light source, but neither melt from sunlight alone.

Snow blocks can be used to make snow golems, but only if you place the jack 'o' lanterns on top last.

35

Even though cacti damage players and mobs that come into contact with them, you can mine cacti with your hand without taking any injuries.

37

The bottom of a cactus block doesn't damage the player – just the top and sides.

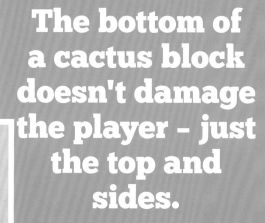

38

Pumpkins are blocks the player can wear. They obstruct your view, but let you look at endermen without provoking them!

39

Melons drop three to seven melon slices when mined, but it takes nine slices to craft a full melon, so it's more efficient to grow melons than to craft them. Melons can't be crafted back into slices – only placed then broken.

40

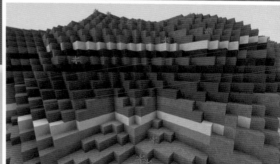

Red, orange, yellow, brown, white and light grey versions of hardened clay generate in mesa biomes. Blue and orange hardened clay generates in desert temples. Magenta, light blue, lime, pink, grey, black, green, purple and cyan clay can only be created by the player.

41

Packed ice looks similar to regular ice, but is opaque and doesn't melt if placed near a light source. Mobs can spawn on packed ice, but not on ice, and you can only find packed ice in the ice spikes biome.

42

Unlike the super-hard block in Minecraft, real-life obsidian is a glass-like mineral that's very easy to shatter.

43

Obsidian and bedrock are the only two blocks to appear in all three of the Overworld, the Nether and the End.

44

Obsidian has a blast resistance of 6,000 (in comparison, stone has a blast resistance of 30), so it's effectively impossible to destroy, although blue wither skulls fired by the wither can destroy it on contact.

45

Sponges are generated only as part of ocean monuments, but can also be dropped by elder guardians.

Once they've taken in water, sponges turn into wet sponges and won't absorb any more water when placed. You can cook them in furnaces to dry them out, so you can reuse them.

46

47

If there's an empty bucket in the fuel slot when a furnace has dried out a sponge, it will turn it into a bucket of water; otherwise, the water evaporates.

TNT explosions can redirect things that are flying through the air, including falling sand and gravel, and arrows.

48

Bookshelves will power up enchantment tables if placed a single block away from them. To make the highest (level 30) enchantments, you need to place 15 bookshelves around the table.

49

50

Bookshelves can be found in strongholds and village libraries, and by trading emeralds with librarian villagers to obtain them.

51

Moss stone found in dungeons, mega taiga biomes and jungle temples is like cobblestone but has green veins running through it and can be used to craft mossy cobblestone.

Stairs aren't just useful for decoration or because they're compact. Walking up them also takes less of a toll on a player's hunger bar than jumping up would.

52

53

On Christmas Eve, Christmas Day and Boxing Day, all chests are given a "present" texture, with either red (single chests) or green (double chests) wrapping paper and a white or yellow bow around the top!

A "locked chest" block that couldn't be opened was generated in every chunk created between 1 and 5 April 2011 and displayed an April Fools' joke if you tried to open it.

54

55

You can place a trapped chest immediately next to a normal chest, which is a good way to maximise storage space.

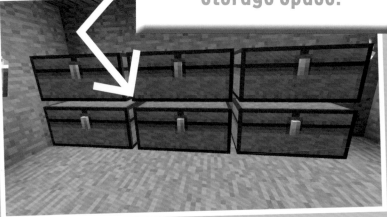

Fences are 1.5 blocks tall so you can't hop over them, but if you place a flat block such as carpet on the top, this will lower the height of the fence so you can jump over it.

56

57

Iron bars (and beds) lower the time it takes a zombie villager to heal. Imprison them in a cell, and feed them a golden apple and potions to begin the process.

58

Four iron bars in a square will create an off-centre gap big enough for the player to drop through, but not large enough for water and lava to flow through.

59

If you break an End portal frame after activating the portal, it won't deactivate, unlike Nether portals, which need a complete frame to function.

Flower pots were added to the game based on a user suggestion. Item frames and ender chests were also created after users requested them!

60

61

Cactus blocks placed in a flower pot won't injure the player and are converted into smaller cacti instead of large, block-sized ones.

62

Prismarine slowly cycles through 22 different colours in a process that takes five and a half minutes to complete.

Nether quartz ore doesn't burn indefinitely and has the same blast resistance (15) as other types of ore, which means it's more protective than Netherrack and pure Nether quartz blocks combined.

63

64

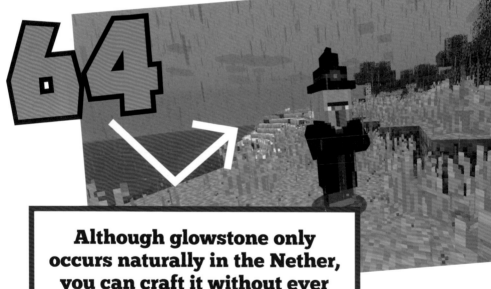

Although glowstone only occurs naturally in the Nether, you can craft it without ever leaving the Overworld as witches drop glowstone dust (which can be crafted into glowstone) when killed.

65

Soul sand suffocates any mob smaller than a slab in height, so it can be used to protect against silverfish and endermites.

66

You can put carpet or snow on top of soul sand to cancel out its effects. Unlike slabs, the game will treat it like you're walking on a normal surface.

Cakes are the only block you can eat. This makes them very easy to store in the Overworld and a great block to use as decoration!

71

Enchantment tables are mostly made of obsidian, so they have a blast resistance of 6,000 and can't be destroyed by TNT.

72

73

Mobs can climb up ladders the same way players do, but they aren't smart enough to stay on them long enough to climb up to the top. You can push them up, though!

You can climb up vines as if they were a ladder, but they don't slow you down when you walk through them like ladders do.

74

75

Ladders and wooden doors are the only wood blocks that can't be used as fuel in a furnace, even though they're made entirely of wood!

76

You can turn stone bricks into cracked stone bricks by smelting them in a furnace.

77

Granite, diorite and andesite are identical to regular stone apart from their appearance. They can't be turned into stone bricks except through the use of a stonecutter in the Pocket Edition.

78

Wherever you place them, vines have a small chance of spreading to a nearby block. They're most likely to spread downwards into air blocks to form dangling vines.

79

Players can see through vines and sugar cane, but mobs can't, so skeletons won't shoot you if you're behind vines and endermen won't teleport towards you.

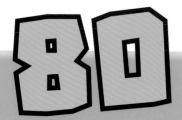

80

You can use bone meal to force sugar cane to grow in the Pocket Edition, but not the PC version.

81

Stained glass blocks have the same properties as regular glass, except they can't be used in recipes that require glass blocks.

82

Hay bales are the only blocks that can be eaten by mobs. They heal up to ten hearts when fed to a horse, donkey or mule, making them the most efficient way to restore their health.

If you fall onto a slime block, you'll bounce and take no damage. You can also put slime blocks under pistons to create a platform that bounces up.

83

84

Redstone lamps switch on instantly if powered by a redstone source, but take 0.2 seconds to turn off when you deactivate them.

85

You can stop the sound from a note block by covering the top of it. This means you can use pistons to mute the sound even though note blocks can't be moved by pistons themselves.

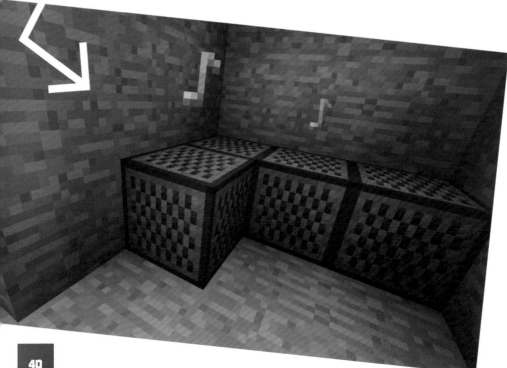

86

Nether bricks can't be destroyed by ghast fireballs, which makes them a good material for building shelters when you're inside the Nether.

87

Monster eggs appear in strongholds and the extreme hills biome. They look like stone, cobblestone or stone bricks (regular, cracked, mossy or chiselled), but break at a different speed to the "correct" type of block.

88

If a silverfish disappears into a block, it will transform it into a monster egg and replenish its health, so don't let it escape!

89

Jack 'o' lanterns can be used to create snow and iron golems the same way pumpkins can.

.90

Glowing obsidian is exclusive to the Pocket Edition and formed when a Nether reactor activates, converting gold into the glowing red, super-hard block.

91

The storage area of an ender chest is different for every player, so you can use them to hide items from other people in your multiplayer worlds.

92

The dragon egg you can collect after killing the ender dragon is the rarest block you can collect in survival mode – there's only ever one per world!

93

Cobblestone walls are slightly lower than fences, so when you connect a fence gate to a cobblestone wall it actually gets positioned lower than if you connect it to a wooden fence.

94

You can craft bricks with a banner to apply a brick pattern on top of the banner in black and white. You can add a dye to change the colour of the pattern too!

Carpets let light through, so you can place carpet on top of glowstone to make a room appear illuminated even if there's no obvious light source.

95

96

You can also place carpet on top of farmland without destroying it, although this doesn't protect it from being jumped on.

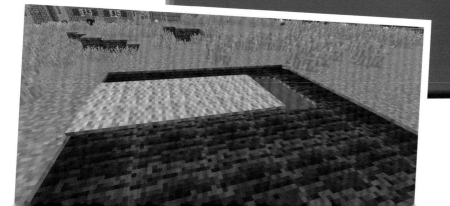

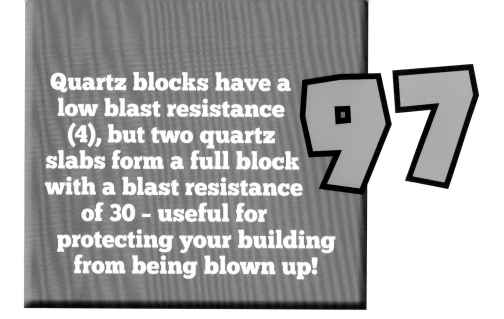

Quartz blocks have a low blast resistance (4), but two quartz slabs form a full block with a blast resistance of 30 – useful for protecting your building from being blown up!

97

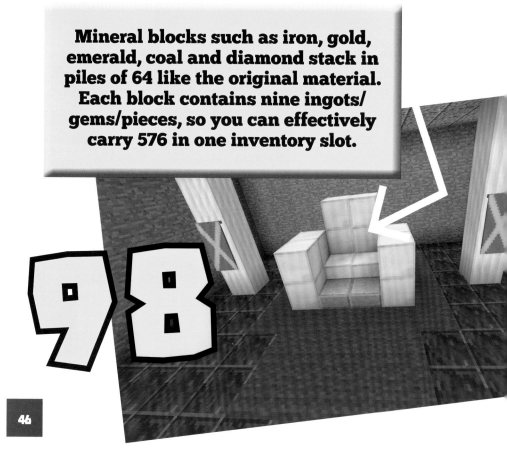

Mineral blocks such as iron, gold, emerald, coal and diamond stack in piles of 64 like the original material. Each block contains nine ingots/gems/pieces, so you can effectively carry 576 in one inventory slot.

98

Coal blocks fuel a furnace for the same length of time as ten pieces of coal, so you actually get a bonus piece for using them as it only takes nine pieces of coal to make one block!

100

99

Using all the different combinations of wood and wool, there are 884,736 ways to craft a bed, but you'll always end up with the same item at the end of it!

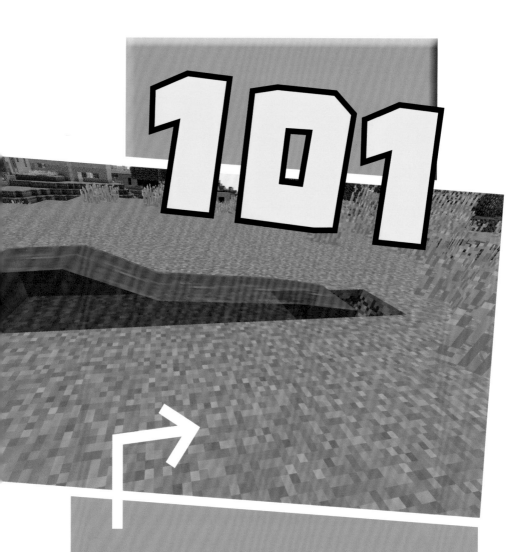

101

If there's a hole within six blocks of a water source block, the flow is directed towards it. Otherwise, it spreads in every direction.

You'll need a bucket to collect lava...

102

Organise your inventory quickbar so that your torches, tools and weapons are within easy reach.

Keep lava buckets around – they're 12 times better than a piece of coal for powering a furnace.

103

104

Iron ingots are very useful – they appear in 27 different crafting recipes, so stock up on them!

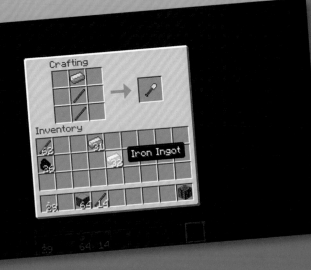

105

You can destroy unwanted blocks by throwing them into lava, into a fire or at a cactus.

Wood is rare underground. You need it to craft many common items, so if you explore a cave make sure to take some logs with you!

106

107

Cooked steak and pork chops are common food items that restore a lot of hunger points. Stock up on them early on!

108

Carry a bed with you so that you can skip nights. But remember, if you die and your last bed is no longer there, you'll be sent back to where you started the map!

109

Don't craft everything straight away. Some resources take up less inventory space than their crafted form (i.e. 1 bone = 2 bone meal). Leaving them uncrafted lets you carry more.

110

Save space by storing ores and metals as blocks. Nine piles of redstone dust can be crafted into a single redstone block, allowing you to carry nine times as much!

111

You can skip storms by sleeping, but while you're asleep crops won't grow and smelting pauses!

112

Blocks will take five times longer to break if you're underwater, but keep your head dry and you can mine at normal speed.

113

When underwater, you can quickly float to the surface by placing a boat in front of you and getting straight into it.

114

If you fall, aim for water – landing in water prevents you from taking damage when falling.

115

When sneaking, it's impossible to fall off cliffs, so if in doubt sneak everywhere!

116

Bunny hopping (sprinting and repeatedly jumping) is quicker than sprinting on its own.

117

Bunny hopping on ice is even faster!

Abandoned mineshafts are a good source of emergency wood if you're trapped underground.

118

119

Stand in a water flow when mining near lava. If you break the wrong block, the water will turn the lava to stone before it damages you.

120 **Never dig directly down! There's no way of knowing if you're above a large drop or a lava lake.**

121

Never dig directly up! Even if you can't see lava or water droplets, there could be a gang of mobs just waiting to drop on you.

122

Try not to dig underwater. It creates a suction current that's hard to swim through and might suffocate you!

123

Boats are much faster than swimming, so use one whenever you can!

124

Fall from a great height onto a cobweb and you'll come to no harm.

Change the colour of a tamed wolf's collar with the use of any dye.

125

Axes aren't just for chopping trees – they mine any wooden block faster than other tools.

Never spend too long underground. When you've collected some resources, turn back and put them in a safe place!

You can cast fishing rods onto pressure plates to set them off from a distance.

129

Put lily pads on water to creating simple bridges – you can walk on them!

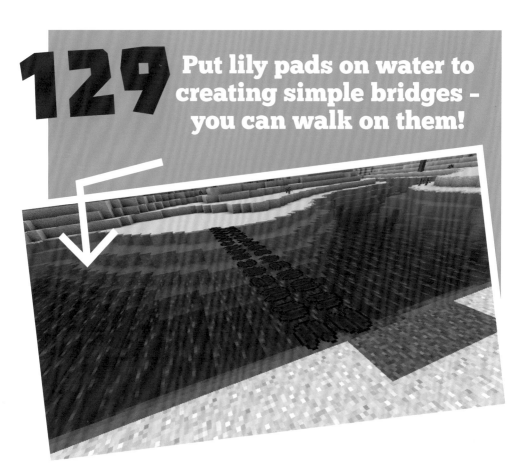

If you're making fences, remember that six Nether bricks will create six Nether brick fences, whereas six sticks will only create two wooden fences.

131

To use less wood, place ladders one block apart - because the player is two blocks high, you'll still be able to climb them as normal.

132

You can use a bucket of water as a portable "elevator". Swimming up and down water flows is quicker than building a staircase!

If you have to fall more than eight blocks distance, teleport using an ender pearl instead and you'll take less damage.

Use doors and fence posts to create underwater "airlocks" that let you breathe.

When exploring underground, only place torches on the right-hand side of a cave. That way, when you want to find your way back to the surface, all you have to do is make sure the torches are on your left!

135

136

Half-size blocks like slabs can be used to create staircases with a more gentle incline than actual staircase blocks.

137

Use a crafting table to encase a piece of redstone in wood and you'll create a musical note block.

138

Wooden slabs are fireproof. Double them up to create fireproof blocks.

Don't use glass blocks as windows. Six glass blocks makes 16 glass panes, so you cover more space using them!

139

140

You can combine lava and water to create cobblestone, stone or obsidian, depending on which of the two are flowing or still.

141

Most ore needs an iron or diamond pickaxe to be mined. Use any other type of tool, and you simply destroy the block without getting anything from it.

142

Dogs catch fire and burn if they get too close to lava!

143

You can often craft four blocks to make nicer-looking blocks: four stone creates stone bricks, and four granite creates polished granite. Try other combinations!

144

Shut villager's doors behind you to keep enemies out.

145

Build a secret escape tunnel out of your home in case mobs block your door!

146

You've a better chance of catching a fish when it's raining.

147

Tamed dogs will attack squid in water!

Cooked meat will replenish more life than raw meat.

148

You can craft mossy stone and bricks by combining vines with cobblestone or stone bricks.

149

150

Destroying a monster spawner gets you the most experience points in the game (other than killing a boss).

151

Feeding sugar to horses makes them heal faster, grow quicker and tame more easily.

152

On a horse, you can run straight over small gaps, and jump over fences and walls.

153

Nether brick fences don't join up to wooden fences, so you can use a Nether brick fencepost to create a gate that lets you through but keeps animals penned in.

154

You can feed tame ocelots raw fish to get them to breed. Use clownfish, as these restore very little hunger and have no other use.

155

You can use a fishing rod to hook animals (and mobs) to lead them around.

Leads allow you to tie up friendly animals so they don't wander off. You can create two leads using four string and one slimeball.

156

157

Witches use a lot of potions. Use a bucket of milk to cure yourself once they've been killed.

158

If you want to keep a zombie or skeleton alive during the day, keep them underwater.

159

Mobs won't cross rails unless they're chasing something, so you can use rails to keep neutral mobs at bay.

160

If a silverfish re-enters a block, it will be completely healed, so don't let them get away!

161

You can cure a zombie villager by throwing a splash potion of weakness at them then feeding them a golden apple. It takes a few minutes!

You can recognise zombie villagers from their faces - they look like green villagers, not regular zombies.

162

You can trap endermen by pushing them into a minecart. They can't teleport away!

163

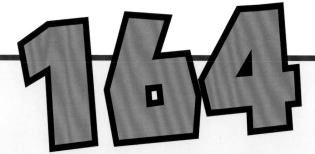

164

You can only find glowstone dust in the Overworld by killing witches.

165

Cauldrons can be filled with water and used to wash the dye off leather clothing, or fill three glass bottles.

166

You can combine enchanted books on an anvil to create books with multiple enchantments.

167

If you're low on weapons, remember that lava can damage most enemies. Keep a bucket handy!

However, fire and lava have no damaging effects on mobs that spawn in the Nether.

168

Bows are good for killing creepers, but endermen will usually teleport away before an arrow hits them.

169

170

If you kill a silverfish in one hit, other silverfish won't come to its aid. Use a diamond sword when fighting them!

You can get lots of experience by fighting blazes. They give 10 experience points per kill, which is at least double that of most others.

171

172

You can heal injured villagers by trading with them or using a splash potion of healing.

173

Wither skeletons can pick up (and use) discarded bows and swords, so don't drop any nearby!

174

Baby zombies are faster and more powerful than regular zombies, so take them out first!

175

When you fight your first blaze, use a golden apple to boost your stats. After that, you can use blaze rods to make fire resistance potions!

176

If you hit an enemy while sprinting, you'll cause a greater amount of knockback. Enough to push a creeper to a safe distance!

You can't eat a glistering melon, but you can use it to create health-restoring potions!

177

178

Lava makes a great (if dangerous) light source. It's one of the few blocks that emits light level 15!

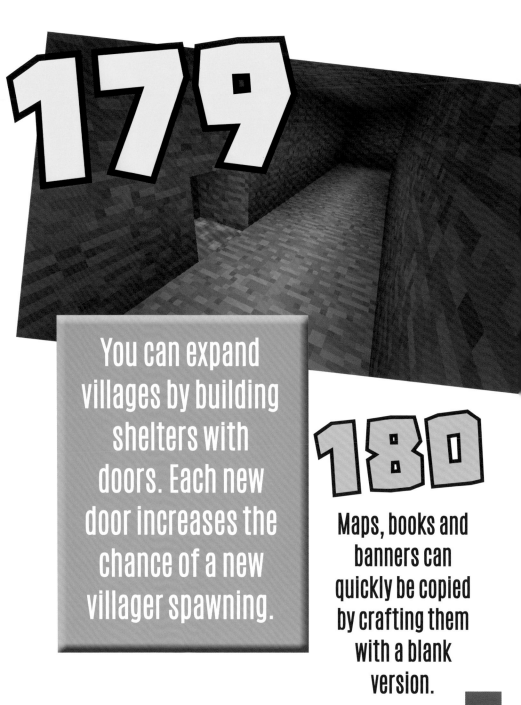

179

You can expand villages by building shelters with doors. Each new door increases the chance of a new villager spawning.

180

Maps, books and banners can quickly be copied by crafting them with a blank version.

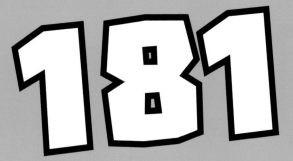

181

You can make it easier to find jungle temples by setting jungles on fire.

182

To play a note block, you can hit it or activate it using a redstone charge. Connect multiple note blocks with redstone to play chords!

The sound of a note block changes, depending on the material it's placed on.

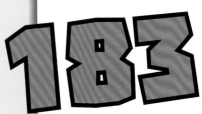

Craft dye with banners to make patterns appear. The position of the dye changes the pattern you see!

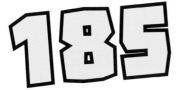

185

Jungle temples are the only place you'll find naturally occurring pistons, levers and dispensers in the Overworld.

You can create an infinite water source with just two buckets of water. Dig a 2x2 pit and place one water source in each corner.

186

187

Minecarts travel fastest diagonally. They travel at eight blocks per second in a straight line, but 11.3 blocks a second diagonally.

188

Riding in minecarts is 10% slower than sprinting, but you can use time travelling to craft or reorganise your inventory.

189

Add extra lighting to villages so that mobs don't spawn inside villager's houses and kill them.

Snow golems can be used as an infinite source of snow. Trap them in a pen or room, and they'll leave snow wherever they walk, which you can then collect.

190

191

Beacons can be built overlapping to save resources, as long as the beacon blocks at the top are at least a block apart.

192

If you build a beacon, place it near your home. This will give you the power-up effects where you need them most.

193

When building redstone circuits, always lay your redstone on easily identifiable blocks, such as snow or bricks. This makes sure you don't accidentally destroy them from another angle.

194

Building a portal in the Overworld will cause zombie pigmen to spawn nearby. Try to build them in a secure room or pit.

195 You can build in the End, but leave the entry platform clear. Anything built or placed on it will be erased whenever someone enters the End.

196 Some blocks behave differently in the End: plants won't grow, compasses and clocks won't work, Nether portals will fail to activate and beds will explode when placed.

197

In strongholds, you can recognise monster egg blocks because they break slightly slower than normal blocks.

198

Minecarts can travel through portals as a shortcut, but remember to protect their route from mobs!

Destroy the pressure plate in desert temples as soon as you find them; otherwise, a mob might spawn and set off the TNT!

199

200

If you repair an enchanted item on a crafting table, you'll lose the enchantment. Use an anvil instead!

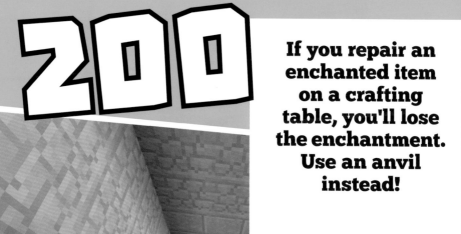

201

The rarest ore in the game is emerald, but you'll only find it in the extreme hills biome. You'll need an iron or diamond pickaxe to mine it.

202

Hide in water to block the effects of explosions from TNT or exploding creepers.